The Young People's Guide to Investing

Simple Guide To Investing For Young People, Millenials, Getting Out Of Debt And Creating Financial Freedom And Independence Early In Life.

Written By
Sam Burchard

TABLE OF CONTENT

CHAPTER ONE:

INTRODUCTION TO INVESTING

Why You Need to Do This Now

By investing early, you are investing wisely. Are you wondering on how to get your hands on $100,000 for your dream business? Or are you looking to visit an African safari on your 25th birthday?

Maybe the plan is retiring by the age of 35, living out of a beach house and opening your laptop a few hours a day to monitor how your investments are doing.

Maybe you still live with your parents and you are thinking that is the least of your problems. Or that it does not really matter at the moment.

But it really does matter.

Those daunting expenses, we associate with adulthood are coming: marriage, kids, a mortage and all those other goodies in between that make life such a paradise.

 Whether you like it or not, it is coming...it is inevitable.

And so, the earlier you start taking investing seriously, the easier it will be to financially secure your future and provide on your dependants too.

Investing is not time-intensive. It is something that you can do if you are still in school or working a full-time job.

There is no license needed and it is not a skill preserved for finance professionals or middle-aged adults. Nobody has an innate advantage over the next person. All you need is the right information.

And with that out of the way, the rest is relatively easy. Every young person is capable of investing and investng profitably. It is not rocket science.

Sadly, most young people do not think about making money. All they do is think of how to spend money, rack up debt and spend even more money. Do not fall into this trap that will eventually swallow most of your high school and college peers.

This book is an investment book which is not exactly a popular topic with young people. However, the fact that you are reading this shows you are thinking of your future and not only what is happening now.

The Investor Mentality

Before you invest, you need to ask yourself 3 crucial questions:

1. Do I have money?
2. How long can I afford to have this money invested?
3. Can I afford to lose money short-term to make money long-term?

Your truthful answers will go a long way in determining if you can do this. In order for you to profit from investing, you need this special kind of mentality—an investor mentality.

This means that as a teenager or young adult you see yourself as someone who makes money and not someone who borrows money. This means you are looking at ways to avoid debt or pay back as soon as you can.

You cannot be a successful investor if you are stuck on a borrower's mentality or incurring debt. If you are in these places right now, you can get out.

But first, let me show you how to develop an investor mentality.

Do You Have the Money to Invest?

When it comes to investing, you need to have money to make money. This comes from you closely looking at your finances—knowing where your money is going and knowing where it is coming from.

In other words, where does your money consistently come from? What are you spending it on? These answers may not come to you all at once. So, settle down, take your time and come to the gradual conclusion, so that you do not forget anything.

You cannot start talking about profiting from investments tomorrow, when you have no idea of where you stand financially today.

If you are making money, the first step is to calculate your monthly income. Keep stock on everything that you get every month.

This goes beyond earning a paycheck. It also includes allowances, bank savings, money gifts from your birthday and so forth. Even if you still take money from your parents, you can add that too.

Once you are done with that, compare it with what you spend every month. How much do you spend on food, music, clothing and date nights? Are you making car payments? Did you make any repairs on the house? Any 401(k) deductions from your payroll?

It may be impossible to keep tabs on all your expenses, but coming up with a majority of it gives you an overall idea of what you have coming in and what you have going out.

Looking at Total Expenses

So what is your monthly income? What are your monthly expenses? After adding up everything is your income and what you save significantly more than what you are spending? If your answer is "Yes" then you are on the right investment track.

On the other hand, if what you spend and what you earn are marginally close...you are not ripe for investing. Not to worry, you are not the only one. A majority of young adults belong in this category...you are not the only one.

So, in order to stand any chance of investing early, you need to get greater value for your spend because that way you spend less. You also need to find ways to whittle down your debts and increase your earnings.

I discuss cool ways to deal with debts and get the best loan deals, later on in this book.

Stay tuned.

Get a Job (Or Get Another Job)

You want to make money? Get a job. If you want to make more money get a job that pays better than the one you are holding right now.

The jury is out on whether young people should be working or facing their books. Some parents fear that teens who get jobs too early abandon college aspirations. Other parents feel it deprives kids of the golden experiences that shape their lives and mould them as human beings.

However, there is always a way to even things out. Even if your parents are providing for you and you work, it means you get to save more money. The more savings you have the more money you have to invest.

I understand that you do not always find your dream job on your first try. But this does not mean you should settle for flipping burgers because it was the only job you could find.

When combing for a job, there are certain things to consider. Of course, the job should be worth your time and pay well. You should also look for something interesting and enjoyable. Thirdly, the job should not interfere with your school or social life.

You do not have to get paid by the hour. So get creative. You can walk dogs, baby-sit or manicure lawns. These jobs do not require professional experience. You easily get to set your work hours and determine how much your time is worth. But be warned, these unconventional jobs are not stable, be prepared to go weeks without something to do if you choose to go this route.

Working for a family member or in a family business is not a bad idea. Just make sure it is worth your time and no one is trying to take advantage of you because of biological ties.

If your job still does not cut it or you are still waiting for the right one to come along, you need to cut down your day-to-day spend In order for you to do this, you need to be frugal. Frugality does not mean you have to be cheap.

Make a list of what you spend monthly. Look for the excesses. Did you buy anything that you could have bought cheaper? How many things did you put on your credit card?

Beware of Plastic Credit

Credit cards may seem like a good idea. However, buying anything on credit as a young person is a habit, you should keep in check. Credit cards are the worst form of debt.

I understand that you are trying to establish good credit—but you need to be careful because it can swallow up your financial life. Borrowing is not something that you cannot totally avoid. You might need to do now or in future. However, as a young adult, I repeat you need to keep it in check.

Buying on credit gives you a false sense of security—that you have money (which actually you don't). Drowning yourself in a sea of debt before you find your feet and spending your productive years trying to pay back is not the right thing to do—it is financial suicide.

Credit cards are card issued by banks after they have agreed that you can pay off the bills you accrue on the card. Credit cards are doled out only if you are 18. And you need to get a blessing from your parents before you get one.

Many parents want their kids to get a card because it is convenient and they believe it teaches them how to be financially responsible. In my opinion, the opposite is always likely the case.

Once approved, your card arrives by mail. As you start to use the card, you get a statement every month highlighting all your purchases. You are faced with 2 scenarios: pay all the money spent or pay the minimum. The statement also tells you when payment is expected as well as the maximum credit you can take.

If you pay back all at once, you are not charged any interest. However, if you opt for only partial payment, you pay back as high as 20% in interest. A growing debt is always terrible crisis. It never goes away and sucks all your finances in the process.

And that is not the only thing to be worried about.

You also end up with a thumbs down credit rating. This ruins your chances of getting substantial loans which can contribute a lot towards your financial future.

Watch Out for Debit Cards Too

Banks give out debit cards. A debit card works like an ATM card and plastic checkbook drawing from your account whenever you need it.

You might not be racking up debt with this one, but this plastic card is also deceptively dangerous. The reason is that you might not really understand how much you have been spending until your bank statement arrives in the mail.

Stay away from these type of cards too. You may not be racking up debt, but you will be spending way more than you should.

One Reason to Love Credit

Inasmuch as I do not support credit cards if you are looking to spend less, I believe they have one super advantage. They are great for building a solid credit rating. But you need to manage your credit card situation well because it can easily spiral out of control.

Here is a smart way that you can get around this—get a charge card. Commit to using this card for a single monthly expense—like gas or your Internet. Charge cards like American Express provide you with short-term credit that must be sorted out at the end of the month.

By sorting out one monthly expense every month, it is easy for you to keep tabs on what you are spending while steering clear of debt issues. This is a smart way to bag a solid credit rating that could come in handy for you.

You Need Good Habits

To have an investor mentality means leaving childish beliefs about money behind. It means keeping an open mind about profitable investment opportunities around you. It means preparing yourself for the unpredictable things—wins and losses down the road.

When you save a dollar, you are not spending it. And not spending it is a conscious decision that you are saving it for something better. Most of the time young people spend money they do not have and spend it on things they do not really need.

Always prioritize what you spend on. This means paying part of your student loan instead of taking a trip to Ibiza. Spending without prioritizing is dangerous.

Control the Impulse to Spend

Are you an uncontrollable spender? You need to figure out how you can peg your impulses. Learn to save money—even if it is a little. Motivate yourself to do this by thinking...emergencies. You must always have money tucked away for the unpredictable curve balls life throws at you.

When you build confidence from doing this, it becomes easy to develop a habit of putting money in an investment account. You are saving before that right investment opportunity comes along. You can do this on a monthly basis or every 3 months.

Inasmuch as you are readying for the future, do remember to give yourself a treat. Nothing over-the-top or dramatic, just you appreciating yourself for the hardwork that you have been putting in.

Do you want to buy a car before you turn 20? Are you planning to skip college and start a personal business? Are you looking to buy a house before your 29th birthday? Plan on retiring by the time you clock 37?

Use these deadlines to laser focus on your financial goals. There is no clear cut route to whatever goal you set. However, remember that your spending decisions play a huge role towards what you can achieve—short term or long term.

CHAPTER TWO: DEALING WITH CREDIT CARD DEBT

3 Major Reasons Why Paying Debt Early is Good

After finishing college, many young people are faced with debt. They are also faced with the difficult decision of either paying off these debts or looking for investment opportunities.

The last time I checked student loan debts had surpassed the $1 trillion mark and it continues to grow. With at least 1 in every 3 loans in default.

I will suggest that you pay off your student loans sooner rather than later.

And here are the reasons why.

Reduced Debt to Income Ratio: When you pay off your debt on time, your monthly payments drop which inevitably lowers your debt to income ratio.

A lower debt to income ratio means you have more income at your disposal. It means you can make purchases, save money and more importantly invest money.

In addition, lenders prefer giving out money to those who have a lower debt to income ratio. You will find it easier to get a loan to buy a house or car, if you go this route.

Pay Less in the End: With time your interests go up. So, the sooner you pay off your loans the better for you in the long run. You do not want to be saddled with a lengthy payback period.

A financial crisis can pop up anytime. You could let laid off or have an unexpected medical emergency. The thing is despite whatever reality throws at you, you are still expected to pay back what you owe.

And delay in payments attract penalties which push you deeper into debt. Do you know you cannot escape your student debt even if you file for bankruptcy?

Boost Your Financial Security: Debt is a threat to your financial security because it keeps on pinching money you should be investing. Once, debt free there is so much that you can do for yourself financially.

With your debt all paid back, you reduce the stress in your life. Constant stress can lead to severe health issues including migraines and heart attacks. So pay back your debt for a peace of mind and good health too.

Imagine this...

You are 25 years old and you owe $5000 on your credit card. And that's just the beginning. The interest rate is 15%. If you make the minimum payment on the card...any guess when you will eventually pay it off?

When you are 47 years old!

This means you will pay $5,729 in interest alongside the principal sum of $5,000 that you orginially owed—an accmulative total of $10,729.

With this illustration, do you see why you need to avoid accumulating debt? No matter, how convenient these credit card issuers make the repayment plan...too much debt is harmful to your long-term financial health.

I understand that not everyone is capabable of escaping from the clutches of debt. No matter how we plan or prepare; life simply happens. So, I understand that debt is unavoidable—whether it is a for tuition or getting a car.

Since debt is unavoidable, the question now turns to how do you manage your debt the smart way? How do you avoid slipping down the rabbit hole? How do you find low-cost loans for a car? So that you do not have to pay back too much? What is the clever way to repay your student loans? While still putting away money for future invesments?

Remember that paying back debts helps build your credit score. This makes you eligible for the best loans. And this comes in handy when the best investment opportunities for you come along.

4 Basic Principles About Credit Debt

Use Savings to Pay High Interest Debt

Always use your savings to pay off your credit cards and pay off other debt with high-interests. Look at it, like this. You owe $1,000 on your card with an annual interest rate of 15% and you have $1,000 in the bank—with an annual interest rate of 1%.

The interest on your $1,000 in the bank is $10. And you have $150 to pay on your card. So what you do is take money out of your savings account and pay off the credit card one-time. You are not earning interest on your savings account. But more importantly, you are paying zero interest on your credit card.

Move Debt from High-Rate to Low-Rate

It is better to pay 8% on interest than to pay 18%. If you have credit card debt that you cannot pay off immediately, get a low-rate card. A card that allows you transfer your current debt, but does not charge you a crazy fee for doing so. This process is called refinancing.

Always Be On Time

Landlords, lenders and even employers always look at your credit history. This says a lot about if you can be trusted to make payments. The number one decider for a great credit score is how often do you pay your bills—on time.

People who are irregular with payments are charged higher interest rates on everything. They can be blacklisted by landlords or employers. You may not be able to turn back the hands of time, but you can turn a new leaf by being punctual with your payments from now on.

Communicate

Let people know that you are more than just an account number. Communicate with your lenders by phone or email if you are trying to get a sweeter deal or sort out a debt-related issue.

Explain your situation and ask politely to speak to a supervisor if you are not getting answers to what you want. I have seen situations where late payment fees have been waived and interest rates lowered just by reaching out.

5 Ways You Can Clear Your Credit Card Debt Faster

If you have credit card debt, the ultimate goal is to clear off your debt as soon as possible. These few suggestions provide you with a soft landing pending when you can get all your debts sorted.

Never Miss Payments

If you cannot make the full payment on your credit card, always pay the minimum at the expected date. Never miss a payment. If you do, then you are charged a late fee. If you default again and again, you get slapped not only with more late penalties, you also have interest rates jacked up. Note that even if you are not charged late fees, your irregular payments show on your credit report.

Know Your Interests

Most lenders use an interest system known as average daily balance method. The issuer divides 12 months into 30 day periods known as billing cycles. If payment is made at the expected date, you do not pay interest. Even if you have $2 left unpaid, it still leaves a negative impression on your next bill.

Pay More than the Minimum

Credit card issuers calculate monthly minimums as 1-2% of your unpaid balance, this includes fees and interest. If you pay only the monthly minimum, you are giving yourself a longer period to sort out your debt. This makes you accumulate plenty of interest along the way. If you cannot pay the complete loan on your card, at least do better than the minimum—it can save you $100s in interest.

Try Secured Cards

If you are having issues getting a credit card because you defaulted on a previous loan or do not meet requirements, there is another option—secured credit cards. With this type of card, you deposit money into a special savings account as collateral.

The issuer then allows you to charge the same amount you have in the account to a secured card. What is the point of this you might ask. Well, it helps you build your credit with more issuers willing to take a chance with you because of your strong record.

Note that secured cards charge higher interest rates than credit cards. You can always compare cards and weigh your options on sites like Bankrate.com and Creditcards.com.

5 Ways to Keep Your Cards in Check

Ask for a Sweeter Deal

Use youth to your advantage. Ask your present company for a better deal. Many card holders who ask for a reduced rate usually get one. Never take everything at face value.

First check for low-rate cards on sites like CardHub.com and Creditcards.com. After that, call the toll-free number on the back of your card and ask to speak with someone in the "rentention" department.

The customer service representative might not have the authority to make a decision. Ask to talk to a manager or supervisor and tell that higher-upper that you would love a lower interest rate on your card.

Tell them that you are thinking about canceling the card because of the high interest rates. Mention the low-rates you found and be prepared to give some names to show you know what you are talking about. Sweetly threaten that you might switch to another carrier unless you get your rates reduced.

Avoid Cash Advances

Most credit cards allow you obtain cash from teller machines. This is not a smart thing to do. Many credit card issuers charge higher rates of up to 24% on cash advances than on purchases.

Moreover, cash advances do not come with a grace period. Your interest starts reading, the minute you get your cash from the ATM. And that is not all, you get to pay a one-time fee for using the ATM or even worse get charged 5% on every amount you withdraw.

Be Careful With Reward Cards

Young people tend to get all crazy about accumulating points for hotel reservations, movie tickets, gift cards and more. But this "free stuff" comes at a price, particularly if you have a debt you are already servicing.

Interest rates that reward cards attract are usually higher than other cards. It is not worth paying the annual fees of a reward card, if you never earn enough points to compensate for the fee. If you are bent on reward cards, go to Creditkarma.com or Creditcards.com to find low fee or free cards.

Stay in Your Lane

Credit card issuers tell you to sign up for overlimits—permission to keep using the card even when you have surpassed your limit. While this might prevent your card from being denied purchases, it is something you do not need.

Card issuers charge as much as $35 for every overlimit transaction. It is never a good idea to use this function even if it makes you look good in front of your friends.

Store Credit Cards

Have you even been asked in a department store if you want to open a store credit account? Retailers will tell you that it gives you a 10% discount on your purchases or something like that.

Do not fall for it.

Interest rates on store cards are through the roof—usually 20% or more. That is way higher than normal credit cards. If you spend $500 on a card and get 10% off and then pay the minimum bill monthly, that still leaves you with an interest of over $200.

That's poor ROI for a $50 discount.

CHAPTER THREE: GETTING THE BEST OUT OF STUDENT LOANS

Basics About School Loans

The average student graduates with over $35,000 in student loans. Most loans come from the Federal government. Federal Direct Loans are the most popular for undergraduate and postgraduate students.

There are also Federal PLUS loans and Federal Perkins Loans made to graduate students and the parents of undergrad students. In addition, there are private loans offered by schools, credit unions and banks too.

There are 2 major differences between federal loans and private loans. First off, federal loans offer lower fixed rates whch can be as low as 3.76% for direct loans. Private students are on the higher side—with 18% or sometimes more.

The second thing is the mcthod of payment. Federal loans have flexible payment plans; which is helpful. Private loans are not so friendly. So stick to federal loans, whenever you can.

3 Ways to Reduce the Cost of Student Loans

Deduct Interest Payments: The U.S. government cuts students some slack when it comes to taxes. This means that you can subtract interest payments on your private and federal student loans by a maximum of around $2,500 every year.

For instance, if you are in the 25% bracket for taxes and you paid $1,500 in annual interest on your loans, you will get apporximately $375 knocked off your tax bill.

Automatic Payments: If you choose to make automated payments from your checking account for federal loans monthly, again the government cuts you some slack. Federal loan servicers whittle down interest rates by a quarter of a percentage point if you pay on time.

Other servicers go lower—half a percentage point. Automated payments ensure you make payments when due and saves you the hassle of cooking up excuses why you miss a payment. Remember this hurts your credit score and deprives you of the best loans which come in handy when the right investment opportunities come calling.

Pre-Pay Loans: If you are not consumed by credit card debt or other loans with high interest, consider jumping ahead of your payment schedule and paying your loans faster.

Paying back loans on time save you interest. For example, let's say you have accumulated $37,000 in student loans with an interest rate of

3.76%. Let's assume that the interest rate does not change and you pay back the amount over the next 10 years.

This means your monthly payment under a standardized plan will be $370. By simply adding an additional $50 to this plan, you pay off your student loans in 9 years—precisely 8 years and 8 months. This saves you an interest of $1,000.

Choosing the Right Federal Loan Plan

If you have to choose a student loan, federal student loans should be your priority. They give you space to breathe with conservative interest rates. This means that you can conveniently pay back your loans and consider investment opportunites as well.

The best place to find a federal loan plan for you is The National Student Loan Data System (nslds.ed.gov). Here, you find all federal loans and the servicers that handle them.

After finding your federal student loan of choice, you are automatically registered in the Standard Repayment plan. In my opinion, this is the best option available because it allows you make the same monthly payment for 10 years.

But what if you are struggling with these monthly loan payments on your entry-level salary? Not to worry, the fact you are automatically enrolled in the Standard Repayment plan does not mean you cannot change your plan to something more manageable.

There is a nifty government tool that you can use called the Repayment Estimator. You can find it here studentaid.gov/repayment-estimator. If you use this handy tool, you will find these alternative payment plans.

Graduate Repayment: The repayment is the same as the Standard Plan—10 years. The difference here is that payments are low and increase every 2 years until everything is paid off.

This is good if the monthly repayment plan is a bit of a stretch for you. But remember that this comes at a cost—higher interest.

Extended Repayment: If you have amassed more than $30,000 in federal loan debt, you can expand payment to 25 years. Payments can be fixed or rise every 2 years.

Monthly payments are lower than the Standard and Graduate plans. And because of this, you end up paying higher interests too.

Income Driven: These plans take into consideration what you owe, what you earn and your income has to be low for you to be considered. If you qualify, you make monthly payments only for a number of years and the government waives the balance of what you owe.

As of the time of this writing, here are the most popular income-driven choices.

Pay as You Earn: This plan comes with the lowest monthly payback plan. After 20 years, your debt balance is waived. Qualifying for this plan is extremely difficult.

Revised Pay as You Earn: The payments here are higher than PAYE. After 20 years, your debt balance is waived. Easier to qualify for this plan.

Income-Based Payback: You make payments for 25 years and after that the remainder of what you owe is forgiven.

These income-plans are short-term options for you to get on your feet when you are not making enough money. As your salary improves, switch back to the Standard plan so that you can service your debts faster and enjoy the freedom of participating in more investment opportunites.

The interest rates on federal student loans are lower than the interest rates on credit cards. Pay off your credit card debt first. If you must, reduce your monthly repayments on student loans to sort out your credit card debts quickly. Once you have wiped off, your credit card debt, you can increase payments for your student loans.

CHAPTER FOUR: GETTING THE BEST OUT OF CAR LOANS

What You Need to Know About Car Loans

You have googled the make and model of a car you want to buy. And you are now shopping for the best deals around in local car shops. You see your dream car, but it is more than what you bargained for and the car dealer offers you financing.

You sign the dotted line...shake hands....deal done.

You are feeling like one smart cookie because you only paid a portion of the initial price and will have the balance payment spread out over a number of years. You might think it is a good deal...but in reality it is not. With financing, a car dealer walks away with more profit than an outright sale.

A car loan is no different. These loans come with higher interests and you are stuck with them. In addition, it is almost impossible to find a lender that will refinance your auto loan at a lower interest rate.

This is why from the jump, you should not only be concerned on the make and model of the car you want to buy, but also where you can get the best loan deals. A 2% rate against a 4% on a $25,000 5-year car loan saves you a whooping $1,300 in interest.

Use the loan savings calculator myfico.com/crediteducation/calculators/loanrates.aspx. With a good credit score, you get lower rates. From my research, you need a credit score of 720 to qualify for the best rates.

Getting the Best Deals

Compare Rates from Banks & Credit Unions: You can get a car loan from a bank or credit union. So, before heading to any dealership go to MyCreditUnion.gov or Asmarterchoice.org and find credit unions offering car loans at low rates.

Once you find a credit union of choice, look for a bank that is willing to cut you some slack, if payments will be taken automatically—most banks will give a 0.1%-025%. If you are lucky, you can get as much as 1%.

Know Price Discuss Financing: The first question a car dealer usually asks is how much can you afford to pay every month. Do not give the dealer an answer right away. Instead, tell the dealer you want to decide on a car first, settle the price and then talk about financing.

Why?

Most dealers try to pull a fast one by extending the payment plan or interest rate for more money. They do this while still trying to match what you are expected to pay monthly.

Haggling is a skill that you have to develop if you want a good deal on a car. Sticker prices are usually 5%-10% higher than what dealers sell. This is known as the factor invoice price. Go to KBB.com and Edmunds.com for factory invoice prices. Aim for 5% and no more. Never pay the sticker price for any car.

Avoid Low Down Payments: The lower your down payment, the bigger the balance and this leaves you with greater interest to pay. If it is something that you can afford, pay for the entire cost one-time. If you cannot do that, fork out at least 20%. And if that is something that you still cannot do, just get a cheaper car.

Buy a Used Car: Getting a used car will save you money. Go for a used car and your car loan will be smaller. Buying a used car comes with plenty of risk. However, there are ways to minmize these risks.

Always ask for a Carfax report when purchasing a used car. This report uses the vehicle's identifcation number (VIN) to collate the car's service and inspection records. With this information, you get the following: title info, mileage estimation, if the car has been in any accident and much more.

Most car dealers provide you with this information for free. You can also get it on your own at Carfax.com for a fee. Never buy a used car without having a competent mechanic inspect it. Never buy a car without appraising the vehicle and taking it for a test drive.

Dealers also sell certified pre-owned vehicles. These are used cars usually under 6 years old that have already being inspected by dealers. CPO cars often have lower mileage estimates than most used cars.

When you get this type of vehicle, it comes with a manfacturer warranty like a new car. Ensure you always read the terms to know what you are getting and what is not covered by the guarantee.

CHAPTER FIVE: 4 INVESTMENT OPPORTUNITIES IN BANKING

As a millenial, your age is a good thing. It gives you freedom to make conservative investments because you have time on your side. And because you are investing long-term, this gives you the room to leverage on compound interests and tax friendly opportunities in banking.

Here are 4 investments in the banking sector that you should consider.

Retirement Investment Accounts: It is not too early to start saving for retirement. Company retirement accounts like 457, 403 (b) and 401(k) are the most common ways to put aside money pending when you want to call it a day from active life.

These retirement accounts do not attract tax until you choose to withdraw the funds—when you have retired. And since you will be a senior citizen by then, you will be paying less taxes.

This a tax break every young adult should consider, particularly when most employers match your contributions with target date funds like the Qualified Default Investment Alternatives (QIDA).

Max out contributions to your investment savings account when you are still single and your family responsibilites are at a minimum. This investing strategy is a good way to help you save more.

High Yield Savings Account: This account is a government-insured savings account where interest rates are higher than normal savings accounts. Depending on market rates and where you look, high-yield accounts can generate 1.5% APY or even more.

Compare this to the average interest for national savings accounts which is 0.97% and you see why it is a good deal. If you leave your money untouched in this account, your account grows without no extra effort on your part.

Here is an example. If you had $10,000 in a national savings account, after a year with a 10% APY, you would have earned just $10. If this money had been left in a high-savings account offering 1.50% annually, your money would have earned a massive 15X times more— $150.

Since 1933, when this was initiated, no one has lost a single cent. Do your homework and sign up only with financial institutions that do not charge you unnecessary fees.

Money Market Accounts: These accounts invest your bank balance in commecial paper, government securities and certificates of deposits (CDs). And because of the moderate risks involved, you earn an nterest.

With this account, you still have access to your money and can withdraw if you want. However, you are given a limited number of withdrawals that you can make in a month. Another good thing with this is that the account comes with a debit card and check writing features. Avoid going below your balance threshhold or you will be fincd.

Mony accounts offer better interest rates than savings accounts but fall short of the returns from CDs. They are good for short-term investments unlike bonds and stocks. Brokerages and retail banking houses are the institutions that usually offer this service.

Certificates of Deposits: A certificate of deposit with a bank is an agreement for a bank to hold on to your money for a reatively long time. It could be 90 days or it could be 6 years. For this action, the bank gives you a higher interest rate compared to what you would have earned on a normal account.

Banks, thrifts, and credit unions offer this serivce to depositors. However, from my experience, online banks offer the best rates beause they do not have overheads to worry about.

Online-only banks like CIT Bank offer irregular time periods like 1
months and not the standard 6 or 18 months traditional institution
offer. If you renege on an agreement and exit early, you forgo
portion of your interest as a withdrawal penalty.

CHAPTER SIX: Getting Started With Stocks

Owning stocks bascially means owning part of a business without the hassles of being part of the day-to-day running of it. As a part owner, you earn dividends when profits are distributed and suffer losses when company's shares take a hit in the market.

Stock prices of viable companies and businesses can be found online, in newspapers or scrolling down the bottom of your favourite news channel. These prices are recorded in dollars and cents and fluctuate every day.

Companies do not control the shares sold to the public. This is handled by a stock exchange. However, the onus is on these companies to determine or influence how their stocks are traded over certain periods.

Here are some common ways that stocks can be sold.

One common way this is done is for the company to buy their stocks like every other investor—a share buyback plan. When a company's shares are scarce, it drives up price.

Secondly, a company can split the stock. Here, the company trades 1 share that has been issued with 2 or more shares of the same. This usually happens when stock price has gone high and is out of reach for small investors—$100 per share is a favored choice for companies considering this.

In 2005, Apple Computer was flying high with the success of the iPod music player. Shares had climbed to an astronomical high of $80 per share. Apple then asked for a 2-in1 split, where everyone who had an $80 share now ended up with 2 shares of $40 each.

Thirdly, is the reverse split. A case where several cheap shares are lumped together for a bigger price. This type of share is often linked to a merger or buyout.

Types of Stocks

To understand the best stocks to trade, we must place them in different categories, namely:

Growth Stocks
Income Stocks
Value Stocks
Cyclical Stocks

Growth Stocks: These stocks are generated by companies with potential growth earnings in future. Investing in these type of stocks require research because they can go up today and suffer a huge decline only days after.

Good research tell you what types of stocks to go for. You can get them relatively cheap and sell them for big bucks in future. In the early 90's, Yahoo and Amazon were just growth stocks, by 1998, prices had gone up by 350%.

Income Stocks: These stocks are the most stable ones around. This stablity guarantees you a consistent flow of income or dividends every year. Examples of companies that sell these type of stocks include: Consolidated Edison, New York State Electric Gas Company (NYSEG) and most U.S. telephone companies.

These stocks give you an over-the average paycheck. Experts might say this does not amount to much. However, if you reinvest your dividends, you make more profits. There is also the possiblity that stock prices could go up and this increases your returns as well.

Value Stocks: Here the company selling stocks is worth way more than the stock price offering. Value stocks do not belong to a specific industry and are way more expensive than they cost.

A value stock has an equal or higher book value for every share than the actual stock price. These are the type of stocks companies with plenty of assets sell. In other words, if the company was broken down and sold in parts, stocks would rise and be equated to book value.

Cyclical Stocks: These company stocks reflect the economic cycles. When the economy is good, stocks rise in price and stakeholders make money.   And when the economy goes south, these stocks dip. Examples of cyclical industries include: real estate, steel, paper and auto manufacturers.

Bring On the Stock Exchange

The most prestigious stock exchange in America is the New York Stock Exchange (NYSE). It was founded in 1792 and is snugly tucked between Wall and Broad Streets in downtown Manhattan, New York.

Trading auctions take place on a centralized floor from 9:30 am to 4 p.m. Eastern Standard Time. Investor representatives also known as exchange members scream buy and sell orders until a price is agreed.

These prices are influenced by the economic laws of supply and demand. With an uptick in demand for a product or service, price increases. And as the demand continues to increase, people are willing to pay more for it. Alternatively, when demand for a product or service decreases, price falls.

In terms of supply, when the product or service increases, price falls. The product and service is easily available and accessible with people looking for bargains, unwilling to pay too much for it. The opposite in this case is lesser supply leads to higher price.

This law of demand and supply also works in the stock market. If millions of people want to sell off their Pepsi shares at the same time, the stock price of this popular drink will take a tumble. On the other hand, if many people want to get their hands on Pepsi shares, then stock shares will rise up because of demand.

CHAPTER SEVEN: PICKING STOCKS & PROFITING

4 Way To Pick The Right Stock

Follow the Trends

To successfully invest in stocks, all you need is the everyday knowledge that most young people usually take for granted. I am talking about industries directed at the youth market. Industries like music, gaming, technology, food, fashion, computers, sports and cars.

Maybe you noticed that a slew of great animated movies are coming from a new subsidiary of Sony. Or there is a new mobile phone game, all teens seem to be playing right now. These are gems hiding in plain sight. As a young investor these are the type of stocks that make you money—if you latch on early.

Be rest assured that whatever is flying off the shelves (or racks) in your city is a reflection of what is happening across the country. So take time to study those ads next time you come across them on your favourite social media.

Parents Also Know What's Happening

Parents are not old school. They also know what is happening—at least in some specific industries. So, leverage on their knowledge when it comes to picking stocks for profit. Imagine if your mother worked in health care and was aware of a new Pfizer drug that cured cancer (just saying!). Or if your dad owned a gas station and knew oil prices were going to go up.

Parents can be a good source of information particularly with topics that literally make us go "yuck". Even if they do not know enough, tell them to help you ask around from their peers and colleagues.

Relax You Have Time

You have time on your side, so avoid investing more than you can afford, particularly if you are still servicing your debt. Risk and reward go hand in hand. This means the more risk you take, the bigger the opportunity to make more money. Alternatively, the less risk you take, the less money you stand to make.

As a young investor, you need to always review your investment goals. How much do you plan to put in? When do you plan to cash out? Look at your risk tolerance, reward and potential for loss. The buck stops with you. You have the youth advantage. This allows you plenty of time to learn and play the market.

You can afford to take conservative risks. You are not a full-blown adult looking to retire in a few years or under pressure to accomplish so much in little time. On the other hand, you can decide to take risks that a middle-aged adult would not take.

You can afford to lose everything before you are 20, learn from your mistakes, come back harder and cover your losses by the time you turn 30. Remember that you cannot totally rely on luck. Research all the time and be convinced by what you have found before making your move.

Let's say you miraculously saved $10,000 before you clocked 15 (miracle? I know). Compounded by a yearly 15%, you can end up with over $500,000 by the time you are 40. If that is $50,000 at the same rate of 15% annually that is a million bucks in 20 years.

Read the News

Take an interest in business news. By doing this, you are most likely to come across an interesting company not many are looking at. It could be a new entertainment company, a cool car or a revolutionary computer screen. When you stumble on these gems, go digging to find out more.

The first place is the local library. Ask the librarian to point you towards information resources. Another good place is the Internet, where zillions of websites reside offering tips and information about potential investments.

The Internet option comes with an advantage, here information is not in hard print and can be easily updated. But you need to be cautious because unverifiable information is bandied across the World Wide Web. Dodgy investment information is one of the quickest ways to lose money.

As a young investor, I suggest that you start off learning about the stock market using resources from the library. After that you can transcend to credible online sources like the ones bellows:

One of my favorite financial portals is MSN Money Central(www.investor.msn.com) Other good sites include Yahoo Finance (finance.yahoo.com), MarketWatch (www.marketwatch.com) and Big Charts (www.bigcharts.com)

Time, Patience and Compounding

Compound growth is the process of earning dividends from your interest. For instance, if you make a 10% annual interest from $10,000, after 12 months that is $1,100. In the 2nd year, another 10% on the $1000 and $100 will give you $1,210 etc.

In 50 years that $1,000 would be $117,391. Imagine if you did that with $5,000...$15,000...$25,000 or $30,000? Remember that as young person you have the time. The question is do you also have the patience.

The law of compound growth despite the low returns is capable of doubling your cash many times over. Unlike Powerball or blackjack at a Las Vegas table, you will surely make profits if you can be patient.

Here is another example comparing your investment with the investment of your parents. Both investments are pegged at 10% interest per year. Let's say you invest $200 monthly from your 15th birthday until the day you turn 35. And then stop putting money and allow the compound interest go to work until you are 65.

On the other hand, your parents invest $5,000 every month and plan on doing so over the next 30 years when they retire. Who do you think wins—this investment battle—you or mum and dad?

You!

When you retire from active life, your total investment of $48,000 would be worth an awesome $2,650,000. Your folks who pumped more money, $360,000 to be exact but who started investing late would have a total retirement amount of $2,260,000. They made just $10,000 more than you. But you invested only two-fifteenths of what your folks did.

The Essence of Dollar-Cost Averaging

Dollar cost averaging is another way to manage your investment portfolio for profits over a lengthy period of time. Here, you religiously make contributions to your investments. Whether it is weekly, monthly or every 2 months.

When you buy shares with a fixed amount, you buy more when the price is low and less when price is high. This keeps your average price low because most of your shares were purchased at lower prices.

This strategy encourages you to invest money regularly for the long haul. And allows you create a solid foundation for your investment portfolio. By simply investing regularly no matter the share price.

Before considering these investment strategies, remember again that great research improves your stock picking and how well they perform. This is not an easy thing to do. If it was easy, we would all be millionaires and lounging in Maldives. Making money is not easy; it does not come to everyone because not everyone is willing to work for it.

Choosing the Right Broker

Large firm brokers are expensive. They have a huge reputation and provide excellent services, but they cost an arm and a leg. To cut costs, you are better off handling the research by yourself.

Large firm brokers charge commissions if they do this research for you and trade on your behalf. Discount brokers like Charles Schwab & Co might be a little bit cheaper, but they still offer the services usually associated with large firm brokers.

Internet brokers are the right fit for young people who want to garner stock trading experience. These brokerages offer the best deals usually 1%-2% less of what large firm brokers charge. While an Internet broker is charging $8-$10 per trade, a discount broker charges $30-$50 for the same trade.

Popular online brokers include Scottrade (www.scottrade.com), Ameritrade (www.ameritrade.com) and E*Trade (www.etrade.com)

CHAPTER EIGHT: MUTUAL FUNDS

If picking winners in the stock market is too much for you, consider this alternative—mutual funds. When you send your money to a mutual fund, it is lumped together with the funds of other investors and managed by a fund manager. The major goal of this manager is to increase the value of your investment with as little risk as possible.

Mutual funds work like the stock market, in exchange for money; you are also given shares. This share price is described as net asset value (NAV) and is determined by dividing the value of your investment by the number of shares purchased.

For instance, Michael Stahl Funds presides over $1 billion in stocks and bonds. If the investors hold 50 million shares in the fund, it means the net asset value of the fund is $20.

The Mutual Fund Advantage

Professional managers do the grunt work. They spend all day looking at stock reports to decide what stocks to add to the portfolio. And because their butts are on the line, if they do not deliver, they do their jobs rather well.

Secondly, mutual funds offer diversification. This is something that you may not be able to do on your own because of your budget. With your money in a mutual fund, which gives you the strength in numbers, your money can be sprinkled into dozens of companies. This means when one company takes a plunge, other companies keep the investment portfolio running.

Thirdly, there is a mutual fund for every goal or any amount of risk you are willing to tolerate. So whatever you are willing to tolerate, there is a fund for you. There are mutual funds that concentrate only on pharmaceutical stocks. Others keep a keen eye only on sport teams like the Red Sox, L.A Lakers and Formula One.

No Load Vs Load

2 ways determine how mutual funds are sold. The commission fee that a broker or financial planer collects is called a load. So a fund that you pay a fee is referred to as a load mutual fund.

Commission vary, but can rise to as much as 8.5%. For example, if you pay $500 into a load fund that charges 8.5% in commission fees, the broker takes out $42.50 and invests only $457.50.

On the other hand, a no-load mutual fund is sold directly with no middlemen and charges zero commission fees. You do make certain payments, but they are not sales commissions. These fees are identifiable and some of them can be avoided if you do not want to pay for them.

Load funds are not necessarily the better option because they charge commissions. And no load funds hold no obvious advantage either, just go with what works for you.

Types of Mutual Funds

Mutual funds gather investments from 1000's of people. This diversity cannot be lumped under a single mutual fund. Below are some of the best mutual fund categories to invest in.

Growth Fund: The objective of this fund is to increase portfolio value by buying stocks that will sell for higher prices in future. With this profit goal in mind, growth funds focus only on established stocks.

Growth funds target companies doing well in their markets or industries. These industries have the tendency of doing better. And this is the reason why their stocks are purchased because they are bound to rise.

Assertive Growth Fund: These funds invest in small and aggressive companies with the confidence that these companies will increase swiftly in value.

Assertive growth funds invest in profitable but high-risk companies. The belief is with high-risk come high-gains. These investments associated with these funds are not around for long. However, a few good returns could have you not bothering to work another day in your life. But be extra careful when you invest in assertive growth funds.

Sector Fund: This type of fund concentrates resources on a single industry. There is a lack of diversity with this type of fund. This explains why it is the most aggressive mutual fund around. This is the fund to use if you are interested in investing only in Microsoft or Pfizer.

It is crucial that you have a good understanding of the industry you choose and understand where standing of the company. If the value of any particular industry is miscalculated, you will lose money.

Income Funds: This mutual fund gives you current income returns. Let's say you invest $1,000 in this fund, you can end up netting up to $3,000, long-term.

Income funds make money by purchasing bonds from corporations or the government. Bonds provide steady income through the interests they pay. Other funds prefer to concentrate only on stocks with huge dividend returns.

I do not recommend this type of fund for a young adult. They are boring and unexciting. With age on your side, you should be looking at more profits, even if it means increasing your risks.

How to Research Mutual Funds

Financial publications like Money, Bloomberg Personal Finance and SmartMoney list top-tier mutual funds and provide updated information about how well they are performing.

The library is another good place to gain access to mutual fund resources: Morningstar's Mutual Funds and The Value Line Mutual Fund Survey. The Morningstar approach is to summarize information about a mutual fund on a single page.

I love it because it comes with a rating system. They assign a star rating of 1-5 (with 5 the highest) for every fund. This rating is based on a prior balance of risk and reward.

The Value Line Mutual Fund Survey is somewhat similar. However, rather than use a star rating system, a number ranking is used based on prior risk and performance.

A rank of 1 indicates the most returns with the least risk, while a rank of 5 indicates the most amount of risk with the least returns. Value Line does one better by providing expenses and even a description of the management style these funds use.

Performance

Performance reports help you decide if a mutual fund is worth all the hassle. And once you are in, it is a great way for you to keep tabs on your investment. However, this should not be the only reason why you choose your investments.

Mutual fund prices are not stable and fluctuate all the time. Always keep in mind that performances should be judged on historical data and not hopeful projections.

The Prospectus

A mutual fund's prospectus grants stakeholders a full disclosure of investment goals and objectives. It highlights the type of securities bonds, stocks, real estate etc owned by the fund and also provides background information of major players on the management team. The level of risk as well as a compact financial statement showing the fund's track record is also there.

A prospectus is written by lawyers, so do not expect it to be an exciting read. However, it is something that you have to do because it gives you a clear perspective of what you should expect. This can save you plenty of pain and money in the coming years.

Always keep an eye out for the minimum investment in a prospectus. It could be as little as $500 or as high as $3000. $3000 may be a difficult amount to come by, so always search for mutual funds that sit well with your pocket.

Custodial accounts offer lower investments than $500, so if you are below 18 and not registered to vote, you can get into this type of opportunity for less money. Make sure the companies mainly invest in slow-growth and low risk companies.

At the back of a prospectus, you will always find historical information and financial highlights of the fund's previous performances. Most funds report performances of 1-10 years.

You should be looking are long-term performances. Any mutual fund can have a good run for 1 or 2 years, particularly if the national economy was booming at that particular time. If you require additional information or require answers to your questions, feel free to get in touch with a representative.

Great Places to Start

Mutual funds are a great place to start investing as a young investor. They are safe and user friendly. Most of them allow young adults to test their strategies with as little paperwork as possible.

Mutual funds provide you with that learning curve needed to build an investment culture from a young age. Conduct your research and come up with conclusions that give you confidence. There is no better feeling than using this research to invest in companies that ultimately succeed.

Conclusion

I hope going through the book has helped you get a better understanding of investing as a young adult. Thank you for reading this book.

www.ingramcontent.com/pod-product-compliance
Lightning Source LLC
Chambersburg PA
CBHW060917130726
48001CB00006B/2285